SCHOLASTIC

News

Nonfiction Readers

D0202016

Let's Talk Swimming

by Amanda Miller

Children's Press®
An Imprint of Scholastic Inc.
New York Toronto London Auckland Sydney
Mexico City New Delhi Hong Kong
Danbury, Connecticut

These content vocabulary word builders are for grades 1–2.

Subject Consultant: Thomas Sawyer, EdD, Professor of Recreation and Sport Management, Indiana State University

Reading Consultant: Cecilia Minden-Cupp, PhD, Reading Specialist and Author, Chapel Hill, North Carolina

Photographs © 2009: Alamy Images: back cover, 4 bottom left, 10 left, 12 (Bill Bachmann), 7 (Corbis Premium RF), 2, 11 bottom (Chuck Franklin); Corbis Images: 13 (Randy Faris), 23 bottom right (Elizabeth Kreutz/NewSport), 9 (Joe McBride); David Madison Sports Images: cover, 1, 4 top, 5 bottom left, 5 top left, 8, 11 top, 16, 17, 20 bottom, 20 top, 21 bottom left, 21 top left, 21 top right, 21 bottom right; Getty Images: 23 top right (Sean Rowland), 5 top right, 15 (Rubberball Productions), 19 (Superstudio); iStockphoto/Gert Vrey: 4 bottom right, 6; JupiterImages/Ron Chapple/Thinkstock: 5 bottom right, 10 right, 14, 18; Masterfile: 23 bottom left; Reuters/Karoly Arvai: 23 top left.

Series Design: Simonsays Design!
Book Production: Scholastic Classroom Magazines

Library of Congress Cataloging-in-Publication Data

Miller, Amanda, 1974–
Let's talk swimming / by Amanda Miller.
p. cm.—(Scholastic news nonfiction readers)
Includes bibliographical references and index.
ISBN-13: 978-0-531-13825-0 (lib.bdg.) 978-0-531-20425-2 (pbk.)
ISBN-10: 0-531-13825-9 (lib.bdg.) 0-531-20425-1 (pbk.)
1. Swimming—Juvenile literature. I. Title. II. Series.
GV837.6.M55 2009
797.2'1—dc22   2008020083

9 10 R 18 17 16 15 14

CONTENTS

WORD HUNT

Look for these words as you read. They will be in **bold**.

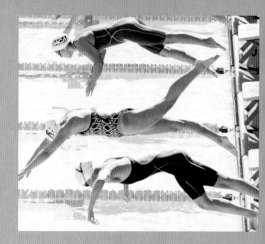

dive
(dive)

kickboard
(**kik**-bord)

starting blocks
(**star**-ting bloks)

4

flip turn
(flip turn)

goggles
(**gog**-uhlz)

stroke
(strohk)

trophy
(**troh**-fee)

Take Your Mark!

A swim meet is about to begin. The swimmers are on the **starting blocks**. This is where the swimmers get ready to race.

starting blocks

The swimmers wait for the sound of a horn to start the race.

The race begins! The swimmers **dive** into the pool.

In most races, the swimmers swim laps. A lap is the distance from one end of the pool to the other.

dive

Each swimmer swims in his or her own lane.

Swimmers move their bodies through the water in different ways. Each way is called a **stroke**. There are four strokes in swimming.

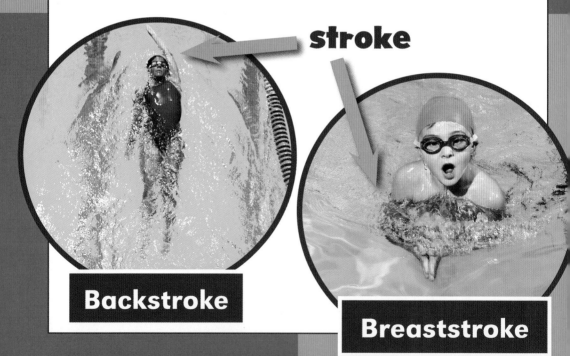

stroke

Backstroke

Breaststroke

Crawl

Butterfly

Kick! Kick! The swimmers kick fast and hard during the race. Swimmers practice kicking with a **kickboard**.

kickboard

A flutter kick is when a swimmer kicks one leg quickly after the other.

Swimmers don't shut their eyes underwater. If they did, they could hit the wall. Ouch! They wear **goggles** to keep water out of their eyes.

goggles

This swimmer wears a cap to keep her hair out of her face.

Swimmers do a **flip turn** at the end of each lap. It's like a doing a somersault underwater! They swim back to the other end of the pool after their flip turn.

flip turn

This swimmer blows bubbles to keep water out of her nose.

These swimmers won the race! Winners get ribbons or medals. The team with the most ribbons or medals wins the swim meet. They may get a **trophy**!

trophy

1.

A swimmer does a flip turn at the end of each lap. As she gets near the wall, she tucks her head down and flips her body underwater. Then she pushes off the wall with her feet. Now she is headed back to the other end of the pool!

6.

FLIP TURN

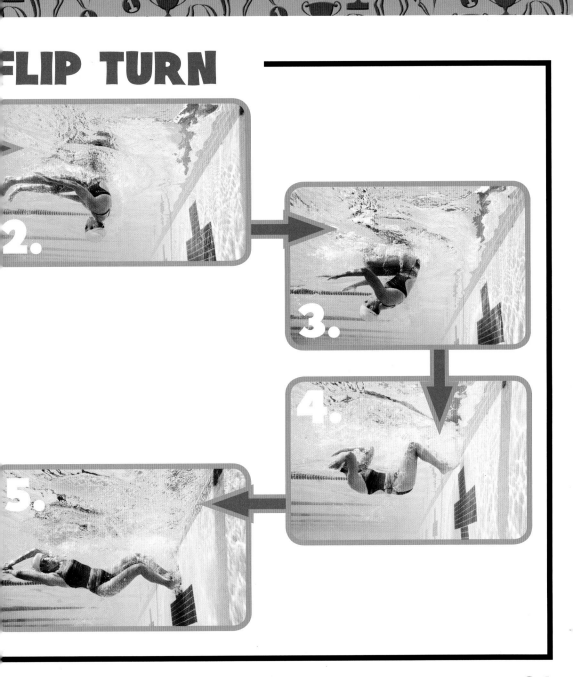

YOUR NEW WORDS

dive (dive) to jump into the water headfirst, with your arms stretched out in front of you

flip turn (flip turn) an underwater action that allows a swimmer to switch direction at the end of a lap

goggles (**gog**-uhlz) special glasses that fit tightly around a swimmer's eyes to keep them dry underwater

kickboard (**kik**-bord) a floating board that a swimmer can use to practice kicking in the water

starting blocks (**star**-ting bloks) raised decks from which swimmers begin a race

stroke (strohk) a way a swimmer moves through the water, such as the backstroke or crawl

trophy (**troh**-fee) a prize given to a winning team

FOUR MORE WATER SPORTS

Platform or Springboard Diving

Surfing

Synchronized Swimming

Waterskiing

INDEX

FIND OUT MORE

Book:
Wallace, Karen. *I Can Swim!* New York: DK Publishing, 2004.

Website:
Splash Zone USA
http://www.splashzoneusa.com/home.html

MEET THE AUTHOR

Amanda Miller is a writer and editor for Scholastic. She swam for the Glendale Gators until she was 12 years old. Now she lives in Brooklyn, New York, with her dog, Henry.